D0462719

ROBERT AITKEN

JAKUSHO KWONG

BERNARD GLASSMAN

MAURINE STUART

RICHARD BAKER

ZEN IN AMERICA

Profiles of Five Teachers

by Helen Tworkov

1989

NORTH POINT PRESS

San Francisco

Cover photographs: Robert Aitken, courtesy of Robert
Aitken; Jakusho Kwong, courtesy of the author;
Bernard Glassman, © Peter Cunningham; Maurine
Stuart, © Julie Thayer; Richard Baker, courtesy of
Jürgen Tapprich. Cover design: David Bullen

LIBRARY OF CONGRESS
CATALOGING-IN-PUBLICATION DATA
Tworkov, Helen.
    Zen in America : profiles of five teachers : Robert
Aitken, Jakusho Kwong, Bernard Glassman,
Maurine Stuart, Richard Baker / by Helen Tworkov.
        p.   cm.
    ISBN 0-86547-354-4
    1. Priests, Zen—United States—Biography.
    I. Title.
BQ9298.T89   1989
294.3′927′092273—dc20
[B]   88-61180

North Point Press
850 Talbot Avenue
Berkeley, California
94706

CONTENTS

ACKNOWLEDGMENTS

When I started off I knew little about how much help I would need and even less about how much help would be forthcoming. In my travels to various Zen centers I was assisted by teachers, guestmasters, cooks, librarians, secretaries, by students who wanted to talk and those who preferred not to. There have been few encounters these past years that have not in ways great and small contributed to this book. My gratitude extends to friends, family, and neighbors in New York and Nova Scotia, and in particular to Anne Aitken, Gary Clevidence, Rick Fields, Norman and Kathy Fischer, Laura Kwong, Lou Nordstrom, Toinette Lippe, to Wally Tworkov for early encouragement, to Pema Chödrön for silent blessings, and to the staff of North Point Press for their support and assistance. I owe special thanks to Nancy Baker, Sheila LaFarge, Larry Shainberg, and Rudy Wurlitzer. More valuable than their editorial help was a persistent faith in this book that held me to it during those times when my own was strained.

In each case the teachers I have written about were completely generous with their time and patience, and their cooperation extended far beyond the requirements of this book. Their understanding of the personal questioning that beleaguered my attempts at objectivity has given me far more than I can return in these pages. In both obvious and subtle ways I owe this book to them. I have done my best to tell their stories, but inevitably they have become my stories. Where discrepancies exist, the responsibility is mine alone.

Much of this work went on at the Zen Community of New York where I have been studying with Bernard Glassman. I am indebted to the membership of this community for standing by my efforts while bearing the brunt of my preoccupations. Once I started this book, Glassman Sensei thoroughly encouraged its completion. But when I first discussed the idea with him, he listened and said nothing. I wish to express my gratitude to him for his guidance in Zen studies and for the wisdom and compassion of that very active response.

ZEN IN AMERICA

INTRODUCTION

"The land of the white barbarians is beneath the dignity of a Zen master," argued Soyen Shaku's monks when Soyen was invited to the World's Parliament of Religions in Chicago in 1893. But the Japanese abbot already had high expectations for the New World. Disregarding the objections of his monks, Soyen Shaku (1859–1919) became the first Zen priest to visit the United States. In Chicago he represented Zen Buddhism with diplomatic discretion. Privately, however, Soyen felt that Zen in Japan had grown impoverished, sapped of true spiritual inquiry. On Soyen's horizon, the future of Zen rested with the barbarians in the West.

In less than a hundred years the United States produced its own generation of Zen teachers, attesting to Soyen's foresight. But the contradictions suggested by Soyen's monks still had to be overcome. Japanese Zen first struck many Americans as indeed too dignified. Compared with casual American behavior, it appeared mannered in the style of aesthetes. From ceremonial tea parties to rigid class hierarchies, things Japanese appeared too close to the old British order that Americans had once rejected. Zen might appeal, as it in fact did, to the intelligentsia, to artists, and to refined New Englanders influenced by the Transcendentalists, but the precise formalities of ancient Japanese customs, all of which are reflected in Japanese Zen, inhibited the possibilities for establishing Zen roots in the United States.

Despite these obstacles, the relative emptiness of the American cultural landscape continued to attract Japanese Zen masters. By the early 1960s Japanese teachers began developing Zen centers in the United States. Although none of these urban centers resembled the mountain monasteries of Japan, their archetype for Zen training—from the environment to interior design, utensils, dress, and personal demeanor—remained firmly rooted on the other side of the Pacific. Then in just one generation, with the passing of Zen from Japanese to American teachers, there was a dramatic change in the accepted look of Zen. By the mid-1970s, converted barns were legitimate meditation halls, scrambled eggs were more common than pickled seaweed for breakfast and most important, Zen teachers spoke English. Only with these obvious transitions did the more profound differences emerge. With the Americanization of Zen, the authority of Japanese tradition began losing ground to the American insistence on questioning tradition. Zen may have made itself at home in the United States, but the process of adaptation has not been easy. At the same time, these abrasions have sparked an inquisitive approach to the ancient teachings that has infused Zen in America with a vitality that has all but been lost in Japan.

When Japanese Zen first came to the United States it was not, as it first appeared, in a tidy package that accurately reflected the larger historical picture of established ideals. It was introduced to the United States by mystical pragmatists and creative abbots who had challenged and changed the Zen system as it was known in Japan. Like that of virtually all the Japanese masters who influenced the course of Zen in the United States, Soyen Shaku's religious training incorporated elements contrary to the monastic conventions of his day. Soyen received his training as a young monk at Engakuji, a prestigious monastery in Kamakura which he later served as abbot. His teacher, Kosen, was the first in Japanese history to combine academic studies with monastic training, thus releasing Zen from its hermetic heritage and paving the way for its move to the West.

Kosen arranged for Soyen's modern education at Keio University, established in 1866 for the study of Western culture—and then sent him to India to study the ancient language of Sanskrit. From there Soyen traveled south to Sri Lanka, where the Theravadin Buddhist monks still followed the mendicant life of the historical Buddha, Gautama Siddhartha Shakyamuni, and his disciples. Soyen wrote to Kosen: "The main purpose for coming to Ceylon is to hide myself from the world of name and fame. Throughout the history of Zen, there have been many teachers who have mingled with beggars, laborers, farmers for the same reason—to hide themselves. I am simply trying to follow their examples in a way that is appropriate to life in the nineteenth century."

By the time Soyen had received his training from Kosen toward the end of the nineteenth century, Zen monasteries had become increasingly co-opted by a wealthy and influential priesthood. While this fortified the religious bureaucracy, the proliferation of temples turned the monasteries into schools for careerists. The quest for temple property and a complaisant life within the priesthood corroded spiritual aspiration. To counter this, Kosen, in addition to providing a secular education for his more astute monks, opened the temple gates to lay students. With their career interests elsewhere, they came to study Zen with no professional investment. This heretical move extended beyond the monastery. In Tokyo, Kosen started a meditation group for lay students called *Ryomokyo Kai*—the Association for the Abandonment of the Concepts of Objectivity and Subjectivity.

Kosen's innovations paid more attention to the spirit of Zen than to the accepted conventions of monasticism, and no one's vision was more instrumental for Zen's transmission to the West than his. For the first half of the twentieth century, Zen activity in the United States was carried out by his lineage alone. Its influence continued through Soyen Shaku's two messengers to the West: the world-famous D. T. Suzuki (1869–1966), who became the popularized voice of Zen, and the little-known Zen saint and monk Nyogen Senzaki (1876–1958).

By orthodox standards neither Senzaki nor Suzuki qualified as a "lineage holder," since neither received formal "dharma transmission," the master's seal of approval to transmit the Zen teachings. This seal authorizes one to be a Zen teacher of the dharma, the Buddhist teachings. "Teaching" and "transmitting" have been used interchangeably, but a distinction is sometimes made between the two terms in an attempt to separate the Western concept of teacher as one who passes information and knowledge from the Zen concept of one who *embodies* the teachings and "transmits" nothing more or less than his own quality of being. In dharma transmission, a master acknowledges a disciple's capacity to "succeed" him in terms of spiritual understanding. The student becomes the teacher's embodiment of Buddhism. In addition, since each dharma heir has theoretically attained his master's understanding, an intimate exchange between master and disciple brings the disciple into direct contact with the realization of Shakyamuni Buddha. Technically, Senzaki and Suzuki represent a break rather than a continuity in Kosen's lineage. They have no place on Zen lineage charts, which list each successive generation of dharma heirs from Shakyamuni Buddha to the present. But whether the transmission of Zen teachings is formally acknowledged, as it was between Kosen and Soyen Shaku, or passed on with no legal seals, as it was from Soyen Shaku to Senzaki and Suzuki, the essence of the transmission system is face-to-face intimacy between master and disciple. Ironically, their lack of pedigree made Senzaki and Suzuki perfect first emissaries to the United States, itself a product of disrupted lineages.

Availing himself of Kosen's program for lay students, D. T. Suzuki lived at Engakuji while attending university. Because he had studied English, he was asked to write the abbot's acceptance letter to the 1893 conference in Chicago. Suzuki, the word-magician of Zen, used language to point the way of no language; to audiences in New York and London he talked about the futility of talk and explained the inadequacy of explanation. For readers, he was the archphilosopher of Zen. For those who knew him, however, his presence authenticated his message. Embodying Zen in the manner of masters, he eliminated the gap between preaching and practicing, and the common failure to achieve this in the West, among clergy or intellectuals, made his presence all the more remarkable. A prolific writer, he attracted some of the most creative thinkers of this century—John Cage, Erich Fromm, Karen Horney, Aldous Huxley, C. G. Jung, Thomas Merton, Arnold Toynbee—and it was mainly through their interest, as well as through the impressions of poets and writers like Allen Ginsberg, Jack Kerouac, and Alan Watts that Zen entered the American landscape. Gary Snyder, the best known of the American poets associated with Zen, also came under Suzuki's influence, and in 1955 he left San Francisco's Beat scene for Daitokuji, a Rinzai monastery in Kyoto.

Through his books, Suzuki set the stage for Zen training in the United States. He suggested possibilities for self-realization that lay beyond the psychological investigations familiar to Westerners, but he did not dishearten his enthusiastic audience with alien rituals and strenuous meditation postures. Missing from his work are comprehensive descriptions of Zen's precise methodology. These methods have been standardized by Japanese customs, whereas Suzuki's concern was to alleviate cultural impositions for his Western readers.

What he emphasized most was the capacity of the mind to attain enlightenment. His own dharma name, Diasetsu, or "Great Stupidity," implies a mind emptied of preconceptions and free, therefore, to experience life "as it is." Emptying the discursive mind is the focus of *zazen*, or "sitting meditation," the foundation of Zen training. The basic radicalism of Zen lies in its insistence on the individual experience of emptying the mind of all personal and cultural descriptions. Dissolving discursive thoughts and stilling the habitual chatter of what Buddhists call "the monkey mind" offer therapeutic benefits. But as a spiritual discipline, zazen not only tames the monkey mind, it channels the religious impulse to surrender the discrete ego-bound mind to the infinity of "skylike" mind.

Suzuki translated the Chinese characters for "skylike" into English as "emptiness." Skylike emptiness implies a boundless state of unity through time and space in which the concepts of objectivity and subjectivity are abandoned. Skylike is so empty, it can receive absolutely everything; it is—to use another translation—"all-encompassing mind." Emptiness is now thoroughly integrated into the English terminology of Zen, but it has generated misconceptions of Zen as a philosophy of nihilism. Yet one empties the small mind not to extinguish one's humanity but to uncover its deepest levels. Releasing what already exists is the process of Zen practice, and it explicitly primes spiritual awakening.

Between the philosophical inquiries spawned by Suzuki and the formal Zen training that soon followed, Suzuki's recurrent references to enlightenment and emptiness led to an unusual chapter in the history of Zen. From the 1930s to the 1950s, Zen traveled a fairly narrow channel in the United States from a recognizable intelligentsia to the avant-garde underground. With the emergence of the Beat generation in the fifties, the emptiness of Zen became a critical reference for a new social iconography. Formal Zen practice was correctly identified with traditional monasticism. But in Beat Zen, form was "square." Only the romance of emptiness was hip. For the Beats all institutions, including those of religion, were rejected for categorically assaulting one's spirituality. The Beats championed the emptiness of Zen as they had American space, an unexplored territory where the past wasn't acknowledged and the future was always in the present. The freedom of mind taught by the Buddhists was confused with freedom from social convention. Life beyond reality, as it was known, was suddenly the only life worth living. Forays into drug-induced enlightenment states did not resemble traditional Zen; but they were often called Zen, and their effect changed America. Zen practice centers eventually transformed much of this fashionable intoxication, but the popularization of Zen lunacy has continued to evoke a faddist curiosity that the practice itself contradicts.

With its focus elsewhere, Suzuki's presentation of Zen delayed the question of how much the methodology should be Japanese—or could be. Japanese monasticism has reflected the same respect for authority, hierarchy, ritual, and circumscribed social behavior that informs all of Japanese life—the very qualities Americans are apt to mistrust most. To what extent the traditions of Zen training are culture-bound and to what extent they uphold the integrity of Zen remains an open question.

Suzuki's dharma brother, Nyogen Senzaki, was the first Zen teacher to suggest to Americans that in addition to dissolving habitual patterns of identification in terms of kinship, status, occupation, sex, religion, age, and so on, ultimately the Zen adept has to let go of ideas of Zen, too. In Buddhist teachings, this dissolution of form into emptiness reawakens the state of original enlightenment. Zen teachings can be used for guidance, but Senzaki made it clear that as concepts, they too have no intrinsic value. The first Zen teacher to take up permanent residence in the United States, Senzaki, like Suzuki, was careful not to introduce too much too soon.

Born in Siberia in 1876, the infant Senzaki was found by a Japanese monk at the side of his mother's frozen body. He came under the care of a Soto priest but was schooled as well in the Shingon faith of his foster father, who also taught him the Chinese classics. Eventually, ill with tuberculosis, he arrived at Engaku Temple to study with Soyen Shaku; during this five-year period of Zen training he also educated himself in Western philosophy. Then, in a move as divergent as his master's journey to Sri Lanka, Senzaki left the temple to start a nursery school in Hokkaido, Japan's desolate northern island. Inspired by the German philosopher Friedrich Froebel, he named the school *Mentogarten*—a place free of any systematized dogma, where everyone could be both mentor and disciple.

In 1905, twelve years after the World's Parliament conference in Chicago, Soyen returned to the United States at the invitation of Mr. and Mrs. Alexander Russell of San Francisco, a wealthy and adventurous couple who had met the abbot in Japan. Senzaki joined Soyen, theoretically to raise funds for his school. But Senzaki had been disgusted with the Japanese Zen establishment and its complicity with the Imperial rule. He had compared Buddhist priests to businessmen, their temples to chain stores, and reviled their common pursuit of money, power, and women. Shortly before arriving in California, Senzaki had spoken out against the militant nationalism that had fomented the Russo-Japanese War and that the Zen monasteries had supported with as much patriotic fervor as the public sector. Exactly what happened between Senzaki and Soyen no one knows. Robert Aitken Roshi, the American Zen teacher who studied with Senzaki in Los Angeles in the 1950s, suspects that although Soyen would never sever ties with a disciple over political attitudes, he did nonetheless disapprove of Senzaki's denouncements. It may be that Soyen asked Senzaki to come to the United States. If this is so, whether it was an act of punishment or protection remains one of several mysteries surrounding Senzaki's relationship with his master.

After working as a houseboy for the Russells, Senzaki made his way alone in California with strict instructions from Soyen not to teach for twenty years. Neither of them ever publicly discussed the intent of this twenty-year ban. Most likely Senzaki had not completed his studies, and Aitken suggests that this stiff sentencing to silence was Soyen's means of instilling, in his own absence, the personal discipline necessary for teaching. As he saw Senzaki off to a Japanese hotel, Soyen told him: "This may be better for you than being my attendant monk. Just face the great city and see whether it conquers you or you conquer it." This was their last meeting.

But whereas Sri Lanka had provided Soyen Shaku with a well-worn path closest to the bones of Buddha, California in 1905 was a Zen monk's tabula rasa, and it tested Senzaki's capacity to invent form from nothingness. He wrote of his isolation and loneliness, of hours spent in public libraries, and of solitary zazen in city parks. For Senzaki the United States was always "this strange land." With little command of English and no professional skills, he worked as a dishwasher, houseboy, laundryman, clerk, manager, and, briefly, part owner of a Japanese hotel. In 1925, the prescribed twenty years over, he began renting public halls in San Francisco with money saved from his scanty wages. In these "floating zendos," as he called them, he talked alternately in English and Japanese. In 1931 Senzaki moved to Los Angeles and opened his Mentogarten Zendo in the modest rooms of his hotel residence in Little Tokyo. There he and his students did zazen on metal folding chairs that he had purchased secondhand from a funeral parlor; sitting cross-legged on the floor in the customary meditation posture struck him as a most un-American activity.

With Senzaki's help, Americans began to learn that although Zen training may tame the mind, it does not necessarily lead to mystical awakening;

but that if the mind can get quiet enough, something sacred will be revealed. The experienced Zen master makes this possibility known by the quality of his own presence. Senzaki assured Americans new to Zen that allowing the unknown to consume the habitual descriptions of reality is the ultimate act of sanity, not a psychotic plunge. Compared to his monastic education under Soyen Shaku, Senzaki's methods were limited. But the ability to let go of self-centered descriptions does not depend on methodology. Senzaki conveyed that while letting go approximates dying, Zen has to do with living. He said of himself that he was "like a mushroom," with no roots, no seeds, no flowers. He wished, at the end, to be blown away like dust. He had none of the quixotic flash of Jack Kerouac or Alan Watts, who by the time of Senzaki's death in Los Angeles in 1958 were generating the Zen boom in San Francisco. He offered Zen training, however rudimentary, when there was little interest in it. He was too "square" for Beat Zen and the Beats had no use for him. "I have neither an aggressive spirit of propaganda," he said, "nor an attractive personality to draw crowds." Purity of heart was his special legacy; with time, it has grown more important.

His isolated and inconspicuous life as a passionate Zen monk in a spiritual wilderness has endeared Senzaki to a subsequent generation of American Zen students. A man of no rank, he disregarded robes and religious titles and wanted only to be, as he put it, "a happy Jap in the streets." Yet despite his mushroom metaphor and the fact that he left no dharma heirs, Senzaki transmitted his realization through two pivotal teachers: Nakagawa Soen (1907–1984), who came to the United States through Senzaki, and Haku'un Yasutani (1885–1973), who came through Nakagawa Soen. These two teachers were trained in the two main schools of Japanese Zen: Rinzai and Soto.

The Rinzai school developed from the teaching style of Rinzai Gigen, of ninth-century China. In his efforts to rid his disciples of their pious idolatry and futile wanderings, he lashed out with nonrational words and gestures and asked questions that stumped the intellect. These encounters evolved into *koan* study. Koans such as "What is the sound of one hand clapping?" and "What was your original face before you were born?" have entered the American vernacular as caricatured examples of Zen at its most enigmatic. Yet while koans are popularly known as "paradoxical questions," they are used to push the logical mind into a realm where no paradox exists.

The Soto school in Japan derived from Eihei Dogen Zenji (1200–1253). Dogen's radical conclusion undercut the rewards of materialistic piety. Zen practice, he said, was not a vehicle for enlightenment but was itself an expression of enlightenment. Undermining the prevalent concept of stages of practice leading to the great liberation, Dogen spoke of the activity of "practice-enlightenment." For him the deliberate striving toward a future goal diffused into the contemplative quality of concentrated stillness in the midst of everyday activity. The Soto way of "gradual awakening" contrasts with the Rinzai emphasis on "sudden enlightenment." According to Soto teachings, one takes a long, slow walk through the morning dew to realize the Buddhist ideal of getting thoroughly soaked by the rains of wisdom. The atmospheric conditions of Rinzai come closer to those of a flash flood.

The Rinzai master Nakagawa Soen's contact with the United States began in 1934 when Senzaki read his poems in a Japanese magazine and initiated a correspondence that lasted for fifteen years before the two men met. Soen completed his university studies in Western and Japanese literature prior to becoming a monk on his twenty-fourth birthday. But like Senzaki, he resisted monastic confinement and divided his time between his temple at the base of Dai Bosatsu mountain and a hermitage on top of the mountain that faced Mount Fuji. When he was at the hermitage, he rose each morning to make prostrations to the sun, then scavenged for berries and edible plants, wrote haiku, and sat full-lotus in the moonlight.

Senzaki collected donations from his students to bring Nakagawa Soen to America. In July 1941 he wrote to the United States consulate general in Tokyo: "Please visa the passport of my Brother monk, Soen Nakagawa." Five months later, the Japanese bombed Pearl Harbor. At the time, Soen was at Ryutaku Temple at the base of Mount Fuji. He remained there throughout the war while Senzaki was interned in Wyoming at the Heart Mountain relocation camp for Japanese-Americans. Since Buddhism had spread east from India to China, and east again to Japan, and then to the United States, Senzaki wondered if the wartime roundup of Japanese-Americans from the Pacific Coast to inland camps was not, in fact, supporting the "eastbound tendency of the teachings." Making the most of adverse circumstances, he called Heart Mountain "The Mountain of Compassion" and named the zendo he started "The Meditation Hall of the Eastbound Teaching." Throughout the war, on the twenty-first day of each month, called Dai Bo-

satsu Day in Japan, Nyogen Senzaki and Nakagawa Soen, with palms to-
gether in the traditional gesture of greeting and respect, bowed to each other,
dissolving the Pacific Ocean between them.

Nakagawa Soen Roshi's first visit to the United States was in 1949. He arrived in San Francisco on April 8th, Shakyamuni Buddha's birthday by Japanese calculations. At a reception at the Theosophical Society library he told
the story of Nangaku, the Chinese Zen master, who was asked by the Sixth
Patriarch, Hui Nêng, "Who are you?" According to Soen Roshi, "Nangaku
was dumbfounded and could not answer. Nowadays, there is no one capable
of being dumbfounded like Nangaku. Everyone knows everything and can
answer any question."

His audience was not dumbfounded like Nangaku. Still, they were
amazed by this tiny Japanese monk, who then reminded them that it was the
two hundredth birthday of Wolfgang von Goethe. He went on to quote
Faust, who lamented that his studies of philosophy, medicine, jurispru-
dence, and theology had made him "no wiser than before," and who con-
cluded, "that we in truth can nothing know."

"This 'we in truth can nothing know,' or 'I don't know anything,'" explained Soen Roshi, "is exactly the point of Zen. We monks apply ourselves
day after day, year after year, to the study of the 'Unthinkable.'"

Soen Roshi had acquired a reputation in Japan for tolerating the casual
interest in Zen of Western students. Gentle and mischievous, he also acquired a more lasting reputation for eccentric behavior. Under his direction,
retreats in New York ended with Beethoven symphonies. Occasionally he
appeared wearing women's jewelry or masks. Once he arranged to have students bow at the doorway of his interview room before they could see that a
pumpkin had been placed on the master's cushion.

In 1962 Soen Roshi canceled an American tour because of his mother's
illness and arranged for Haku'un Yasutani to replace him. Three years later,
Yasutani Roshi became widely known to Americans through *The Three Pil-
lars of Zen*, compiled and edited by Philip Kapleau Roshi. The first Western
publication to concentrate on Zen training, the book opens with Yasutani
Roshi's lectures to beginning students. These were derived from Yasutani's
master, Dai'un Harada Roshi (1871–1961), long considered the regenera-
tive force of Soto Zen in this century.

In an attempt to revitalize Zen in an age of degeneration, Harada Roshi devised introductory talks to inspire the modern mind. Students in the West take this format for granted, but it was heterodox in Japan, and Harada was sharply criticized by his conservative peers. There the traditional training of a novice monk was deliberately devoid of verbal instruction. Paying attention, listening, and what Zen calls "being mindful" were both methods and targets of practice. Even more disturbing to Soto officials was Harada's incorporation of Rinzai koan study, effectively used to shake out the complacency that can creep into the Soto way of "just sitting."

Yasutani studied with Harada on the rugged coast of Japan's inland sea for twenty years, receiving at the age of fifty-eight his master's approval to teach. Shunning the Zen establishment, Yasutani then removed himself to a small rural temple, Taiheiji, in the outskirts of Tokyo, where students lived in their own residences and continued their regular employment. At Taiheiji he founded the *Sanbo Kyodan*—the Order of the Three Treasures—an organization that attributed to lay students the kind of worthy intention Zen orthodoxy had reserved for monastics.

Yasutani used combative tactics in the zendo that reflected the Rinzai methods incorporated by Harada into Soto training and were further intensified by the limited time allocated for lay practice. He made no concessions to Americans new to Zen, running his zendo in the militaristic style associated with Japanese samurai. Exhorting retreatants to break the barriers of conceptual thought, Yasutani projected a battlefield that pitted the forces of ignorance against the forces of enlightenment and urged his troops to "attack the enemy." When testing students individually, however, he probed, questioned, and analyzed every nuance of an answer, disabusing anyone of the notion that a Zen master could not hold his own in Western dialectics.

In Japan the association of Zen with the samurai tradition sanctioned it as a masculine ideal, but in the United States in the early sixties the nonaggressive activity of zazen initially attracted mostly women. While intellectuals, both male and female, approved of reading about Zen, for the time being American men were not to be found sitting still on a cushion apparently doing nothing. What appealed to many women was the affiliation between Zen and the refined arts of calligraphy, ceramics, tea ceremony, and flower arranging. And the style of Zen training did nothing to dispel this. There is nothing gaudy about Zen meditation halls. Notoriously neat and clean, they feature simple altars with few images; the incense is not overpowering and the flower offerings are limited to one or two elegant arrangements. Of all the Asian disciplines to come to the United States, Zen alone augmented the Anglo-Protestant legacy of aesthetic classicism and suggested a gentility and aristocratic grace that affirmed ancestral tastes. This aesthetic validation was more apparent on the East Coast, which remained largely unfamiliar with the racial prejudice that had plagued Oriental laborers in California. New England had long enjoyed an influx of Oriental art objects imported through the Boston-based East India Trade industry; and influenced by the Transcendentalists as well as the Unitarians, educated people in the Northeast were generally familiar with numerous Oriental texts in translation.

For a segment of New England's sophisticated upper class, and particularly for women, Zen aesthetics legitimized an attraction to Zen practice. Not only did this influential elite gain approval for Zen on a larger scale, but by the mid-1960s it was providing solid financial patronage for some teachers. Yet in the process of stimulating a favorable climate for Zen in the United States, the meeting between the puritan legacy and Japanese Zen aesthetics also kindled some tenacious misunderstandings. Puritan simplicity evolved from moral, not artistic, discrimination. The association between refinement and moral rectitude is American, not Japanese. Aesthetic austerity has differed widely in these two cultures. In Japan it was cultivated for sensual pleasure; in the United States it was intended to retard sensuality and, specifically, sexual response, the asceticism of the Shakers being an extreme example. Japan is not a puritanical culture, and so it is ironic that the first patrons of Japanese Zen in the United States were the direct heirs of puritan values.

When American definitions of morality are applied to Zen training as measures of approval or censure, a kind of cultural gridlock occurs in which the integrity of both systems remains obscured. This conflict, which has yet to be resolved, was not addressed directly until 1983, when at Zen centers in Los Angeles and San Francisco the moral behavior of the teachers was openly questioned by students and publicly documented. The public charges, similar to private allegations leveled at other Zen teachers, American and Japanese, included drinking and sexual misconduct. Underlying these denunciations was the fundamental question of the spiritual authority of the Zen teacher. Rooted in Zen history, this line of inquiry ultimately confronts the enigmatic domain of the Zen adept.

Zen evolved in China in the seventh century in defiance of the scriptural authority established by the existing Buddhist schools. The try-it-and-see-for-yourself method advocated by Shakyamuni Buddha had degenerated into memorization and repetition of holy texts. Repudiating mimicry and idolatry, Zen masters said things like: "Buddha is a shit stick!" "If you meet the Buddha, kill the Buddha!" "Don't look to me to get enlightened!" Responses like these have continued throughout Zen history, contributing to its eccentric reputation. But for all its apparent iconoclasm, knocking Buddha-images off their pedestals was meant to restore faith in personal experience. "Look within," said Shakyamuni. "You are the Buddha," Buddha meaning "awakened one."

When Zen developed in China, the Confucians were the arbitrators of moral probity. The specialty of Zen masters resided in guiding the disciple beyond mental realities, beyond cultural and moral biases. Their domain was, as Nakagawa Soen said, "the Unthinkable." To forge a discipline for the attainment of the unthinkable called for revisions within religious structures; but behavior allied with the unthinkable did not threaten social cohesion, nor was it provoked by social disintegration.

In the United States the attraction to Zen training was prompted by a decade of moral confusion. The election of President John F. Kennedy promised a cultural reawakening that came about only with the violence of the Vietnam War. With the help of consciousness-expanding drugs and Eastern religions, members of the counterculture pursued personal transformation with a vengeance. Zen studies combined the individual quest for spiritual guidance with a need for a new social morality, and Zen teachers were delegated the moral roles of American clergy. Yet American moral codes and the traditional authority of the Zen teacher are not always compatible. Trying to bring them into alignment has, thus far, proven a stumbling block to acculturation. For the jurisdiction of the Zen teacher finally to come under scrutiny indicates just how far Zen has dug its roots into the grit of American habits. The mystique of Zen, which initially inhibited the investigation of traditional practice, was subsequently used to protect an idealized version of Zen training and Zen teachers. With the recent questioning of spiritual authority, the romantic era of Zen in America has come to an abrupt close.

Challenging this spiritual authority could not begin until there were American teachers and students matured in their practice. Japanese Zen masters had arrived from a culture long considered exotic, spoke little or no

English, and were reputed to embody spiritual wisdom—to be living masters—a phenomenon for which white America has no indigenous reference. Glamorized, the authority of the Zen master went unquestioned. To examine its exact nature was inadvertently to admit that no remarkable experience had occurred that was profound enough to silence all the unaskable questions. In the heady ambience of Zen circles, this was tantamount to personal failure on the part of the novice. To embrace the authority of the master with blind devotion, on the other hand, was just as often considered an indication of spiritual insight. The result was a perverted glorification of Zen. In addition, Americans simply did not know how to think about living masters or their spiritual traditions in human terms. Only with the appearance of American teachers did the mystique of Zen become sufficiently neutralized to allow basic questions to emerge. What does it mean to call someone a fully realized Zen master? What is enlightened behavior? Who is enlightened and how does one know? What, if anything, can the unenlightened mind use for measurement and assurance? Is there any view that is not culturally biased? There are no absolute answers, but it took a quarter of a century of Zen practice before Americans could even begin asking the questions.

For the teacher, spiritual autonomy is rooted in Zen orthodoxy and validated through the system of dharma transmission. The Zen lineages now in the United States trace their descent through eighty to ninety sequential generations of Buddhist patriarchs back to Shakyamuni Buddha.* According to texts written after the Buddha's death, the first transmission occurred when Shakyamuni, sitting before his assembly, twirled a flower. In response, his disciple Makashapa smiled. On the lineage charts, the first six names are mythological Buddhas who represent beginningless time. Shakyamuni Buddha is the seventh and Makashapa the eighth. No seals, signatures, or papers verified Makashapa's understanding. Presumably Makashapa's smile conveyed the same quality of skylike mind as Shakyamuni's. At that point, the boundaries of dualistic perception abandoned, there was no teacher or dis-

*There is a recent tendency in the United States to replace the word "patriarch" with the ungendered "ancestor" when referring to Zen. The change reflects the participation of American women in Zen and accurately communicates that Zen is not for men only. But the elimination of the term "patriarch," particularly with regard to lineage, denies the masculine dominance of the tradition and the fact that none of the teachers listed prior to the current generation has been female.

ciple, no object or subject, nothing taught, nothing to teach. This unified state of skylike mind remains the ideal archetype for Zen transmissions.

Makashapa's is the simplest transmission story ever told. In Japan, as Zen developed an extensive religious structure, transmission became increasingly shrouded in the kind of mysterious religiosity that Shakyamuni Buddha and the Chinese Zen masters had originally rejected. Dharma transmission in Japan became confirmed in a secret week-long ceremony culminating in a midnight ritual and witnessed by a few select clergy. What happened between Shakyamuni and Makashapa, however, is never openly revealed either. Truly mysterious by nature, dharma transmission remains self-secret, unknowable however public it may be. This dimension of transmission is indicated in a famous Zen quote attributed to Bodhidharma, the first Zen patriarch of China:

> A special transmission outside the scripture
> No dependency on words and letters,
> Pointing directly to the mind of men,
> Seeing into one's nature and attaining Buddhahood.

Bodhidharma's direct teaching was a blasphemous affront to scriptural authority. The ruling priesthood in turn attacked his heretical claim, but what evolved as the Zen school legitimized itself by asserting that its "special transmission" descended directly from the historical Buddha. Historians now suggest that this direct descent is somewhat fictional, that the lineage charts list consecutive names of masters who lived hundreds of years apart. Zen protectors may have resorted to a kind of written validation similar to the scriptural authority they attacked. Perhaps the claim for an unbroken lineage enabled Zen to attract some of the Imperial patronage enjoyed by the prevailing Buddhist schools. Perhaps claiming direct descent from Shakyamuni was a skillful attempt to establish the viability of these radical teachings in a conservative and antagonistic climate.

In any event, the system of transmission became increasingly corrupt as Zen became more institutionalized. Dedicated masters from the time of Dogen Zenji ranted against the self-serving abuses of dharma transmission. But appeal to personal probity still remains the only recourse for protecting true transmission, since the self-secret aspect of the system allows for every possible pitfall. Whether transmission is between Shakyamuni and Makashapa or between some scurrilous father and son scheming to keep temple property in the family, the paradoxical integrity of the system is that there are no external references, no objective tests or measurements. It is a kind of Zen honor system which, by human law, will inevitably be defiled.

When defiled, transmission became something "to get," "to have," "to possess," a kind of religious credit card that proclaimed authority and guaranteed respectability. Transmission certificates were obtained through bribery and forgery and given liberally by abbots to their eldest sons to assure family ownership of temple property. During the nineteenth century, the abuses of transmission accelerated the decline of Zen in Japan.

When Yasutani Roshi and Soen Roshi traveled around the United States in the 1960s, no one knew or asked about dharma transmission. Shunryu Suzuki Roshi (not to be confused with D. T. Suzuki), who founded the San Francisco Zen Center in 1962, never mentioned it. But by the early seventies, while many Americans were already studying with Asian teachers, many more were facing a perplexing array of guides and gurus. The "guru circuit" was derisively compared to a spiritual marketplace, but where aspiration outlasted curiosity, there was genuine concern for what defines a legitimate teacher. Centers for disseminating Asian religious teachings were sprouting up all over the country, and competition for students and financial support was considerable. For some new spiritualists, implicit trust in a teacher made "proof" of authenticity irrelevant. Others, however, felt inadequately qualified to assess spiritual attainment. Within this confusing proliferation of New Age alternatives, Zen offered dharma transmission as a system of certification by which authenticity was not sanctioned by personal opinion but screened and confirmed by one experienced in spiritual matters. That only the ideal version of transmission was presented to students new to Zen was not a promotional falsehood. Until recently, it was the only version available.

The Japanese Zen teachers may have underestimated how their idealistic American students would respond to the dilemmas of dharma transmission. In Japan, the so-called impurities of Zen culture came with the territory, and deviations from the ideal did not diminish or threaten the pursuit of Zen for dedicated aspirants. But open-hearted American students of Zen have been altogether a little naive about spiritual matters.

One common misconception in the West is that spiritual realization diminishes—if not altogether eradicates—the personality, a view that assumes similarities and reduces differences between dharma teachers. Yet throughout Zen history the individuality of the great masters suggests that long after the layers of ego-protection have dissolved, the attributes of personality will flourish and particularize the teachings. For this reason, masters themselves speak of "Dogen's Zen," "Rinzai's Zen," "Ikkyu's Zen," and so on. Zen teachers have singular personalities and individuated teaching styles, and they present their understanding of Zen in very different ways. Shakyamuni Buddha's enlightenment remains the model of an awakened mind, but in Zen history there is no one behavioral ideal against which lesser gods are measured. Without objective measurements, one person's genuine master is another person's spiritual fake. There is no system, no gauge, no test that will change this—nothing to relieve the personal pursuit of what is real, what is true. Yet the Japanese system of dharma transmission continues to provide useful guidelines from which to explore possibilities of Zen studies.

When I first conceived of this book in 1984, there were seven Americans whose qualifications for transmitting Zen had been acknowledged by their Japanese masters and who were independently teaching Zen at their own centers. Five agreed to be interviewed for this book. Since then, this first generation of American teachers has doubled in size. In addition to the Zen derived from Japan, Zen is being conveyed to Americans by Chinese, Vietnamese, and Korean masters, and in some cases by their American successors. There are also American teachers of Buddhist traditions other than Zen. Concentrating on Americans within the Japanese Zen tradition, however, makes it possible to trace patterns of cultural adaptation. Americans were involved with Japanese Zen earlier and more extensively than with other forms of Buddhism, and it is now evident that the difficulties of assimilation go beyond individual teachers, centers, and lineages and are generic to acculturation itself.

These five American Zen teachers present their own understanding of Zen—not American Zen, not Japanese Zen. The transformation into a truly American version of Zen will evolve with successive generations of practitioners, teachers, and students. As a Buddhist expression puts it, "When the student is ready, the teacher appears." Yet it is incumbent on the teacher to manifest spiritual insight in a form that is recognizable to the student. These first

American teachers have appeared under unique circumstances. Their historical position requires considered distinctions between the traditional styles of Japanese Zen and the essential spirit of Zen teachings. At once bearers of the old and pioneers of the new, they must withstand the fragmentation of tradition and the reinvention of form and arbitrate the possibilities for continuity through trial and error. Each of these teachers is currently engaged in new directions, experiments, or major ventures. All their choices are themselves the transmission of Zen and contribute to the ongoing translation of Zen into an American vocabulary. And while their individual teaching styles are distinct voices engaged in a common search, at this time there is nothing that can properly be called "American Zen."

Master Sekiso said, "How will you step forward from the top of a hundred-foot pole?" Another eminent master of old said, "Even though one who is sitting on the top of a hundred-foot pole has entered realization, it is not yet real. He must step forward from the top of the pole and manifest his whole body throughout the world in ten directions."

What does "the top of a hundred-foot pole" mean? Figuratively, it is the stage of complete emptiness. When you attain self-realization, your eye will open first to the state of consciousness where there is absolutely nothing. That stage is called the "great death." It is a stage where there is no dualistic opposition such as subject and object, good and bad, saints and ordinary people, and so on. There is neither one who sees, nor anything seen. Zen usually expresses this stage with the words, "There is not a speck of cloud in the spacious sky."

Anyone who wants to attain the true Zen experience must pass through this stage once. If you remain there, however, you will be unable to attain true emancipation from deep attachment to this emptiness. This stage is often referred to as the pitfall of emptiness. It becomes a kind of Zen sickness.

When we attain kensho, we come to the top of the high pole where most of us are seized with this malady. It is said that even Shakyamuni succumbed to it for two or three weeks after his great enlightenment. The Zen master in this koan warns us not to linger at this point when he says, "Take a step forward from this stage, and you will be able to manifest your whole body throughout the world in ten directions." That means that you must become completely free from all kinds of attachments.

Yamada Koun

ROBERT
AITKEN